# MICROSOFT WORD



KABIR DAS

# Contents

CHAPTER I

# MS Word?

Microsoft word is a word processor software developed by Microsoft in 1983. It is the most commonly used word processor software. It is used to create professional quality documents, letters, reports, resumes, etc and also allows you to edit or modify your new or existing document. The file saved in Ms Word has .docx extension. It is a component of the Microsoft Office suite, but you can buy it separately and is available for both Windows and macOS. The latest version of Ms Word is 2019. In this article we will learn the features of Ms Word, but first we learn how to open Ms Word?

## *The following step shows how to open MS words:*

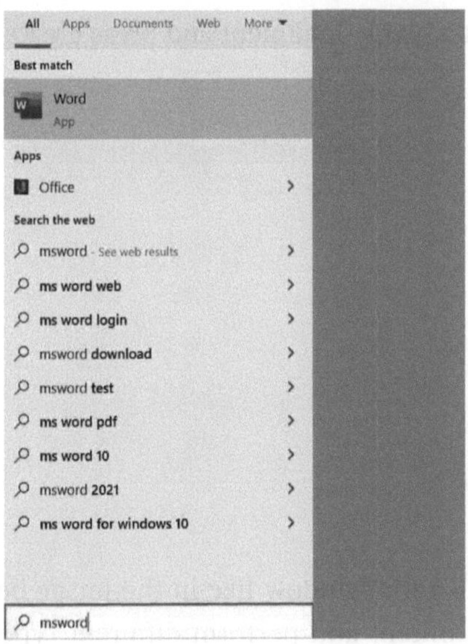

Step 1: Type Ms Word in the search bar.

Step 1: Type Ms Word in the search bar.
Step 2: Select Ms Word application.

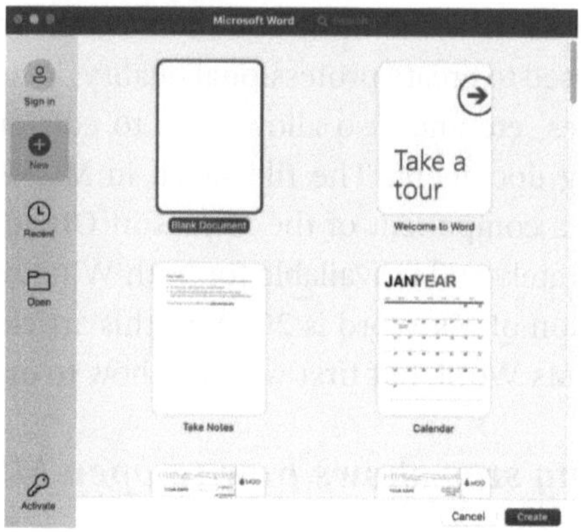


Step 3: Select a blank document and press create button.

Step 3: Select a blank document and press create button.

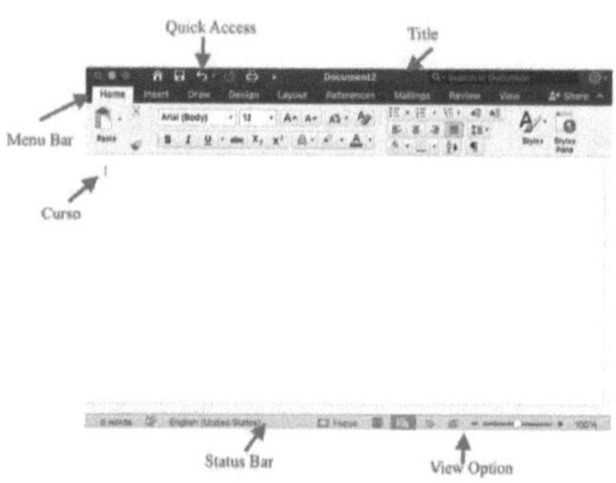


Then you will get a window like in the image below where you can write your content and perform different types of operations on that content, like font type, style, bold, italic, etc. You can also add images, tables, charts to your document.

## *Features of MS Word*

Now let us discuss the features or components of the Ms Word. Using these features, you can perform different types of operations on your documents, like you can create, delete, style, modify, or view the content of your document.

1. **File**
   It contains options related to the file, like New(used to create a new document), Open(used to open an existing document), Save(used to save document), Save As(used to save documents), History, Print, Share, Export, Info, etc.

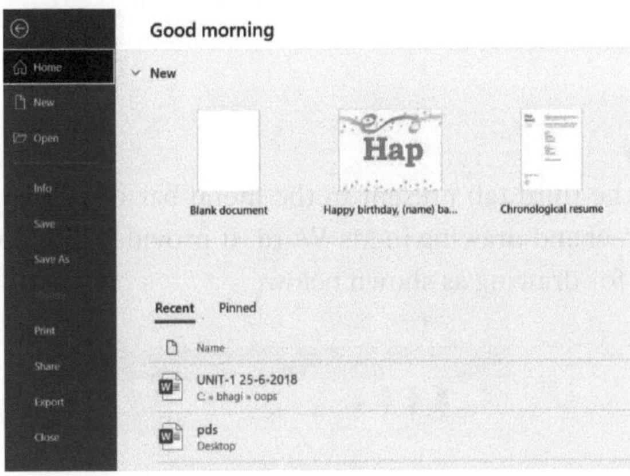


2. **Home**
   It is the default tab of Ms Word and it is generally divided into five groups, i.e., Clipboard, Font, Paragraph, Style and Editing. It allows you to select the color, font, emphasis, bullets, position of your text. It also contains options like cut, copy, and paste. After selecting the home tab you will get below options:

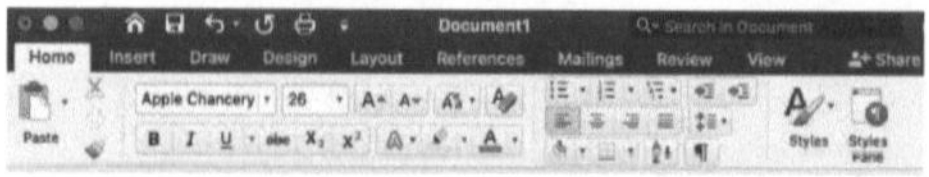


3. **Insert**
   It is the second tab present on the menu bar or ribbon. It contains various items that you may want to insert into a Microsoft word. It includes options like tables, word art, hyperlinks, symbols, charts, signature line, date and time, shapes, header, footer, text boxes, links, boxes, equations, etc., as shown in the below image:

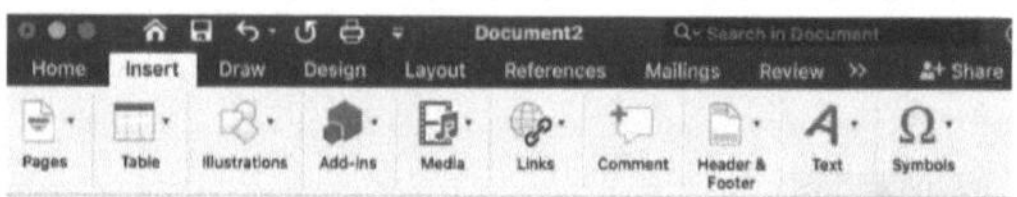


4. **Draw**
   It is the third tab present in the menu bar or ribbon. It is used for freehand drawing in Ms Word. It provides different types of pens for drawing as shown below:

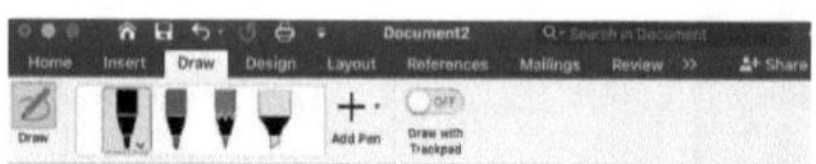


5. **Design**
   It is the fourth tab present in the menu bar or ribbon. The design tab contains document designs that you can select, such as documents with centered titles, offset headings, left-justified text, page borders, watermarks, page color, etc., as shown in the below image:

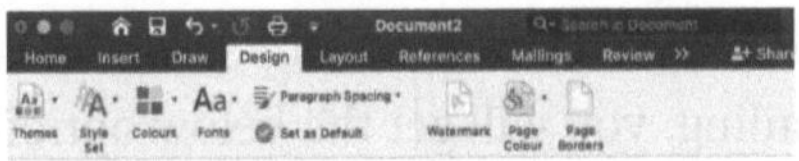


6. **Layout**
   It is the fifth tab present on the menu bar or ribbon. It holds all the options that allow you to arrange your Microsoft Word document pages just the way you want them. It includes options like set margins, display line numbers, set paragraph indentation, and lines apply themes, control page orientation and size, line breaks, etc., as shown in the below image:

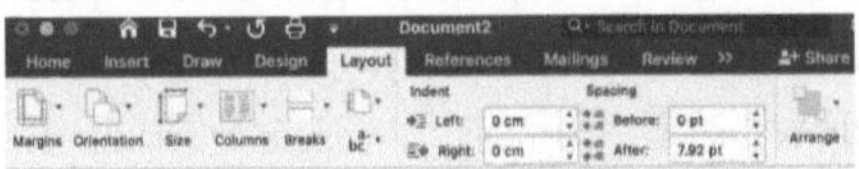


7. **References**
   It is the sixth tab present in the menu bar or ribbon. The references tab lets you add references to a document, then create a bibliography at the end of the text. The references are generally stored in a master list, which is used to add references to further documents. It includes options like, Table of Contents, Footnotes, Citations & Bibliography, Captions, Index, Table of Authorities, smart look, etc. After selecting References tab, you will get the below options:

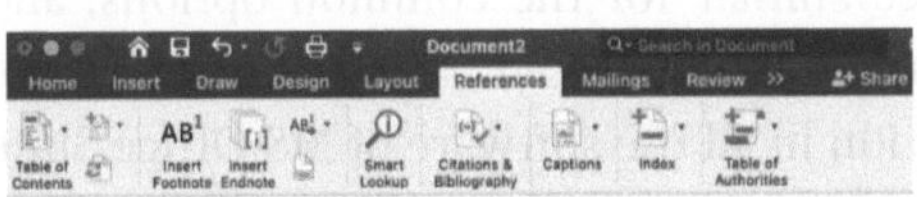


8. **Mailings**
   It is the seventh tab present in the menu bar or ribbon. It is

a least used tab in the menu bar. This tab is where you would create labels, print them on envelopes, do mail merge, etc. After selecting mailing, you will get the below options:

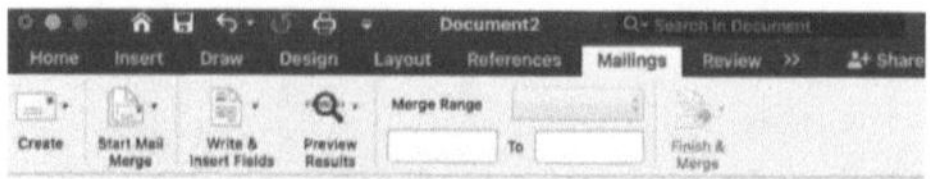


9. **Review**

   It is the eighth tab present in the menu bar or ribbon. The review tab contains, commenting, language, translation, spell check, word count tools. It is good for quickly locating and editing comments. After selecting a review tab, you will get the options below:

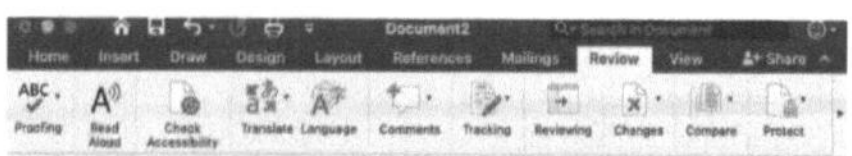


Microsoft Office or MS Office Suite is an all-in-one package of several programs that help us perform most office-related tasks, such as creating documents, spreadsheets, presentations, databases, etc. Some of the essential software programs of MS Office Suite include MS Word, MS Excel, PowerPoint, etc. To make all these software user-friendly and effective, Microsoft tries to make the user interface similar for the common options, allowing users to find commands and tools with ease. Office button is one such common option in all the software of MS Office Suite 2007.

In this article, we are discussing the Microsoft Office button (also called the Office button). The article also concludes the function of the office button along with the options listed under it.

## *What is an Office Button?*

The office button is an essential element of Microsoft Office Suite 2007. This button was introduced in Office 2007 with the new Ribbon feature. When we click on the Office button, it displays some useful options which are used very frequently. Specifically, the Office button provides us options to open, save, print any document, or perform other common functions. Additionally, the office button allows us to configure the preferences or settings of the particular Office product.

The office button found in MS Office 2007 products looks like this:

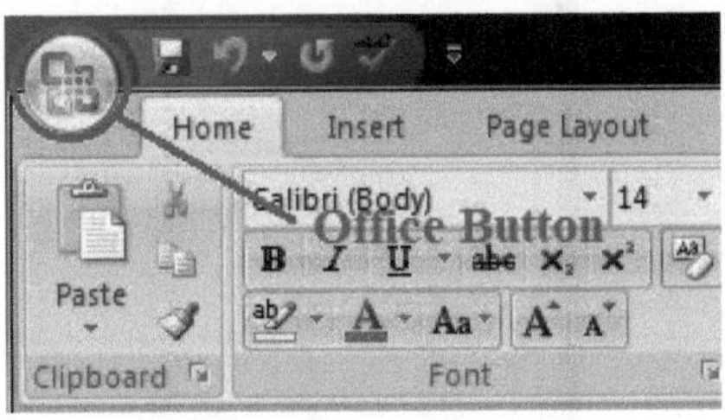


## *Where is Office Button found?*

The office button is located on the top-left corner of Office 2007 programs, namely Excel, Word, PowerPoint, etc. The button is attached with the ribbon and is identified by a circle containing an Office logo inside it.

Office Button Menu Options

The following options or commands are displayed when we click on the Office button:

- New: This option allows us to create a new, blank file in the corresponding Office program, such as MS Word, MS Excel, PowerPoint, etc.

- Open: This option allows us to open an existing file from the local storage on our computer.
- Save: This option allows us to permanently save a temporary file to our computer after finishing the work. Additionally, we can save the changes to the current file using this command.
- Save As: This option allows us to save a copy of the active file with the desired file name and file extension to a desired location on the computer storage.
- Print: This option allows us to take a hard copy of the desired document on paper through a printer. Alternately, the print option can help us save a copy of the active document to a PDF format.
- Prepare: This option allows us to prepare the active file for distribution. In particular, the prepare option helps us view and modify the document properties accordingly. Furthermore, we can also inspect the hidden metadata of a specific file using this option.
- Send: This option enables us to send or share the desired files directly through the opened Office program with others. In particular, we may share active documents by e-mail, upload them to OneDrive, or post to a specific blog. The send option is renamed as 'Save and Send' in Office Suite 2010.
- Publish: This option enables us to distribute the desired document to people. We can even create a specific blog article with the content inside the file.
- Close: This option helps us to close an active document in a corresponding Office program.

**Quick Access Toolbar**

Quick Access Toolbar lies next to the Microsoft Office Button. It is a customizable toolbar that comes with a set of independent commands. It gives you quick access to commonly used commands such as Save, Undo, Redo, etc.

When you click the drop-down arrow next to toolbar it offers more commands. With a left click you can add any of these commands to Quick Access Toolbar. You can also remove the commands added to the tool bar. The indent, spacing values, individual styles and other features that appear on the ribbon cannot be added to quick access toolbar. The following image is showing the menu of quick access toolbar.

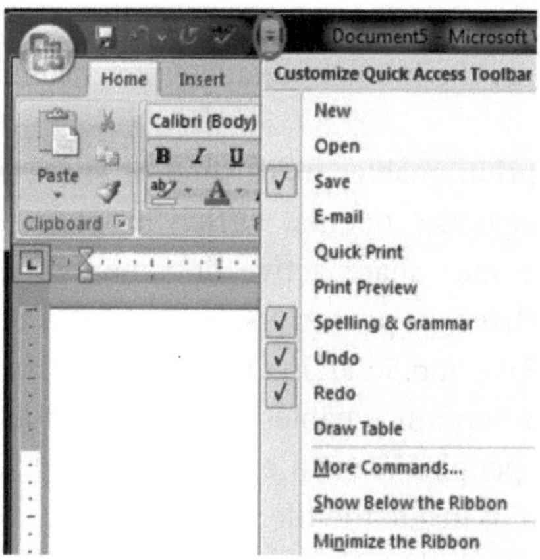


It lies next to the Quick Access Toolbar. It displays the title of the currently open document or application. It is present on almost all windows displayed on your computer. So, if there are several windows across the screen, you can identify each window by looking at the title bar. In many graphical user interfaces, you can also move a window by dragging the title bar.

**Ribbon and Tabs**

The Ribbon is a user interface element which was introduced by Microsoft in Microsoft Office 2007. It is located below the Quick Access Toolbar and the Title Bar. It comprises seven tabs; Home, Insert, Page layout, References, Mailing, Review and View. Each tab has specific groups of related commands. It gives you quick access to the commonly used commands that you need to complete a task.

- **Home tab:** The Home tab is the default tab in Microsoft Word. It has five groups of related commands; Clipboard, Font, Paragraph, Styles and Editing. It helps you change document settings like font size, adding bullets, adjusting styles and many other common features. It also helps you to return to the home section of the document.

- **Insert tab:** Insert Tab is the second tab in the Ribbon. As the name suggests, it is used to insert or add extra features in your document. It is commonly used to add tables, pictures, clip art, shapes, page number, etc. The Insert tab has seven groups of related commands; Pages, Tables, Illustrations, Links, Header & Footer, Text and Symbols.

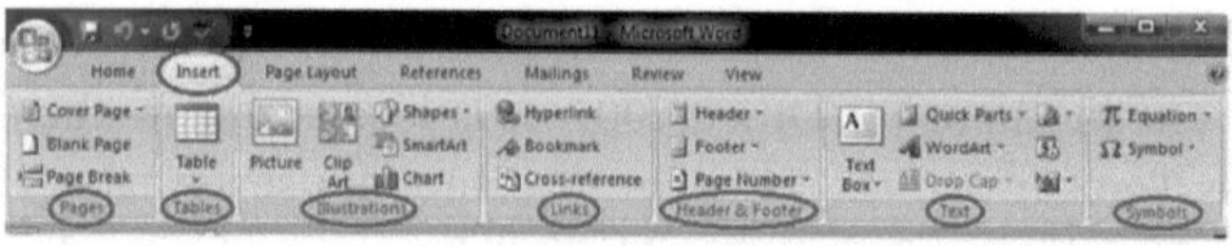


- **References tab:** It is the fourth tab in the Ribbon. It allows you to enter document sources, citations, bibliography commands, etc. It also offers commands to create a table of contents, an index, table of contents and table of authorities. The References tab has six groups of related commands; Table of Contents, Footnotes, Citations & Bibliography, Captions, Index and Table of Authorities.

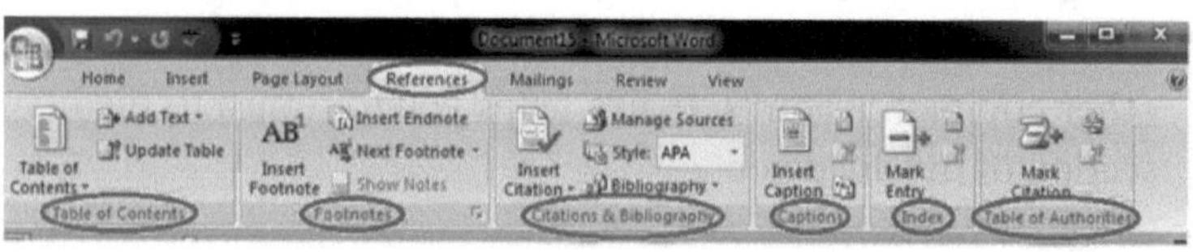


- **Mailings tab:** It is the fifth tab in the ribbon. It is the least-often used tab of all the tabs available in the Ribbon. It allows you merge emails, writing and inserting different fields, preview results and convert a file into a PDF format. The Mailings tab has five groups of related commands; Create, Start Mail Merge, Write & Insert Fields, Preview Results and Finish.

- **Review tab**: It is the sixth tab in the Ribbon. This tab offers you some important commands to modify your document. It helps you proofread your content, to add or remove comments, track changes, etc. The Review tab has six groups of related commands; Proofing, Comments, Tracking, Changes, Compare and Protect.

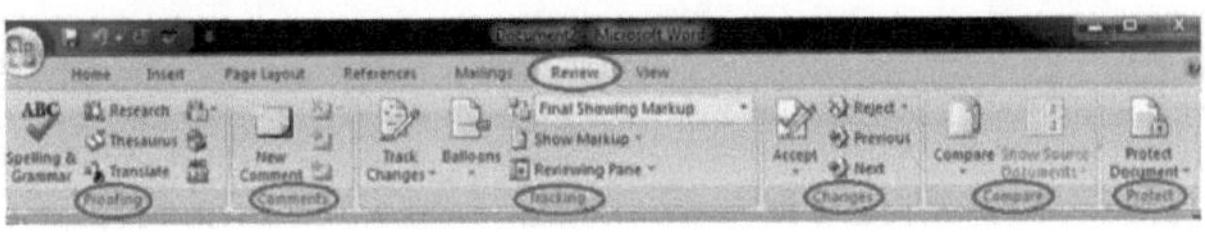


- **View tab:** The View tab is located next to the Review tab. This tab allows you to switch between Single Page and Two Page views. It also enables you to control various layout tools like boundaries, guides, rulers. Its primary purpose is to offers you different ways to view your document. The View tab has five groups of related commands; Document Views, Show/Hide, Zoom, Window and Macros.

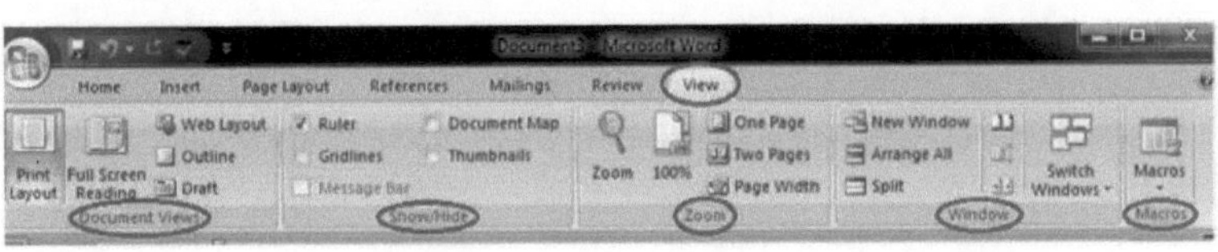

### Ruler

The Ruler is located below the Ribbon around the edge of the document. It is used to change the format of the document, i.e. it helps you align the text, tables, graphics and other elements of your document. It uses inches or centimeters as the measurements unit and gives you an idea about the size of the document.

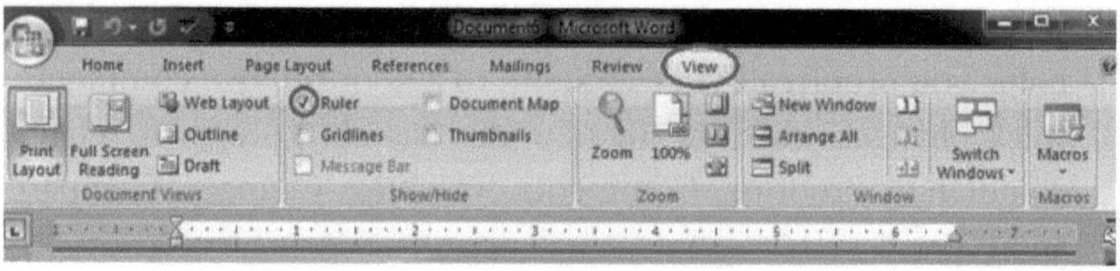

CHAPTER II

# Text Basics

**How to Insert Text in MS Word**

The basic steps to insert text or to create a new document in Word are listed below;

- Go to the start menu and look for Microsoft Word icon
- Click the icon to open the Microsoft Word
- You will see a blinking cursor or insertion point in the text area below the ribbon
- Now, as you start typing, the words will appear on the screen in the text area
- To change the location of insertion point press spacebar, Enter or Tab keys

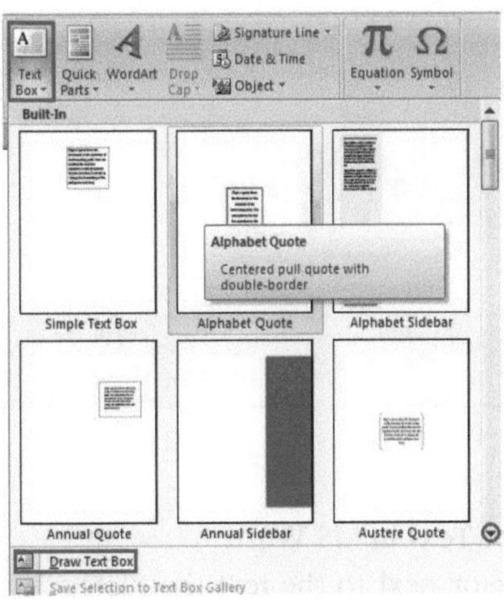


**How to Delete Text in MS Word**

You can easily delete the text in Word including characters, paragraphs or all of the content of your document. Word offers you different methods to delete the text; some of the commonly used methods are given below;

- Place the cursor next to the text then press Backspace key
- Place the cursor to the left of the text then press Delete key
- Select the text and press the Backspace or Delete key
- Select the text and type over it the new text.

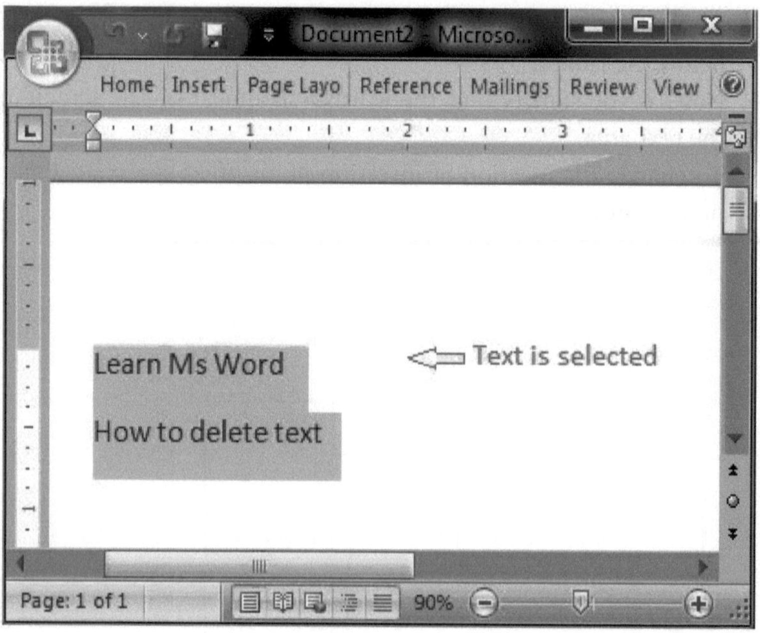


**How to Select Text in MS Word**

Place the cursor next to the text then left click the mouse and holding it down move it over the text then release it. The text will be selected.

Some shortcuts for selecting text are:

- To select a single word double click within the word
- To select the entire paragraph triple click within the paragraph
- To select entire document, in Home tab, in Editing group click Select then choose Select All option or press CTRL+A
- o Shift + Arrow; hold down the shift key then press the arrow key, the word will select the text in the direction of the arrow key. There are three arrow keys, so you can select the text in three different directions.

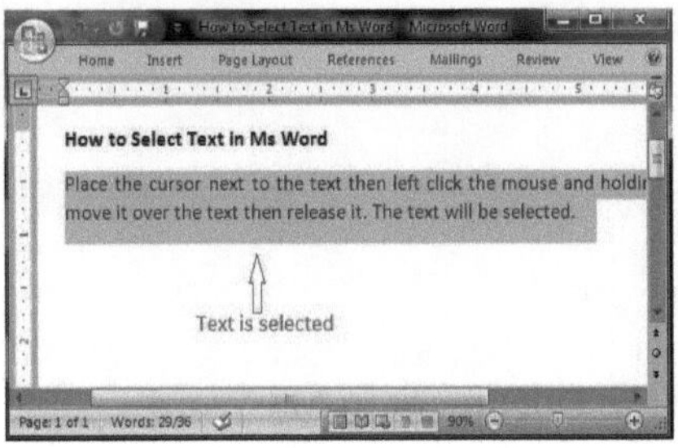


**How to Copy and Paste Text in MS Word**

Word offers different methods to copy and paste text. Some of the popular methods are given below;

Method 1;

- Select the text you want to copy
- Select the Home tab and click the Copy command
- Place the cursor where you want to paste the text
- Click the Paste command in Home tab

Method 2;

- Select the text
- Place the cursor over the text and right click the mouse
- A menu will appear; with a left click select the "Copy" option

- Now, move the cursor to a desired location and right click the mouse
- A menu will appear; with a left click select the 'Paste" option.

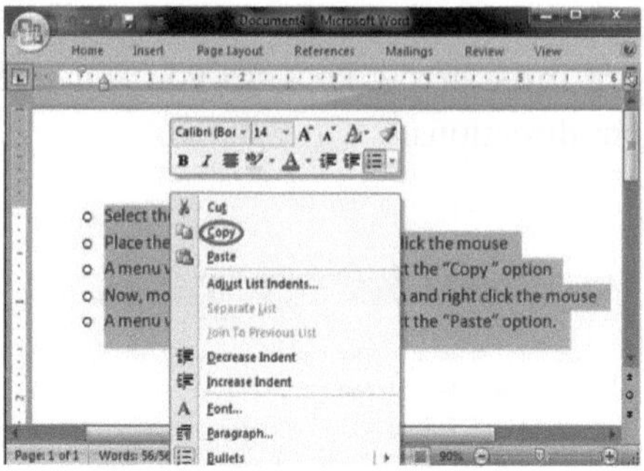


**How to Save the Document in MS Word**

When you create a document it is important to save the document so that it can be viewed or reused later. The basic steps to save a document are listed below;

- Click the Microsoft Office Button
- A list of different commands appears
- Click the 'Save As' command
- it displays 'Save As' Dialogue Box
- Save the document to desired location with a desired name

You can also choose 'Save' command from the list to save the document to its current location with same title. If you are saving a fresh document it displays 'Save As' dialogue box.

The shortcut method to save a document is to press "Ctrl+S" keys. It opens the 'Save As' dialogue box where you can name you document and save it to a desired location.

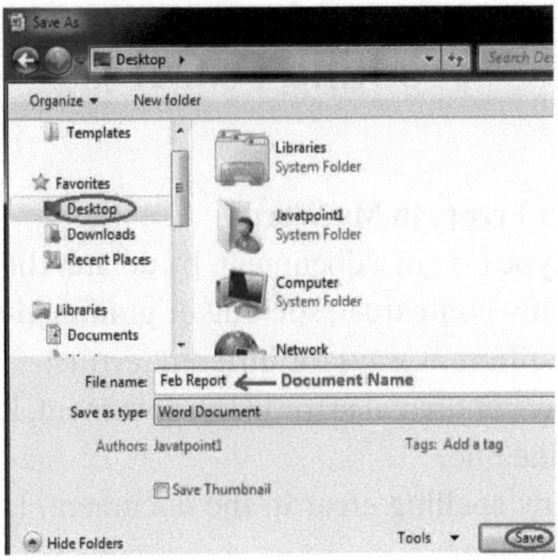
Save As
Desktop
Organize
New folder
Templates
Favorites
Desktop
Downloads
Recent Places
Libraries
Documents
Libraries
System Folder
Javatpoint1
System Folder
Computer
System Folder
Network
File name:
Feb Report
Document Name
Save as type:
Word Document
Authors:
Javatpoint1
Tags:
Add a tag
Save Thumbnail
Hide Folders
Tools
Save

CHAPTER III

# Proofing Features

## How to Correct Errors in Ms Word

When you type text in a document, by default the Word informs you if there is any contextual, spelling or grammatical error. Word informs you in different ways for different errors;

If there is any contextual error in the document, it will underline the text with blue line.

If there is any spelling error in the document, it will underline the text with red line.

If there is any grammar error in the document, it will underline the text with green line.

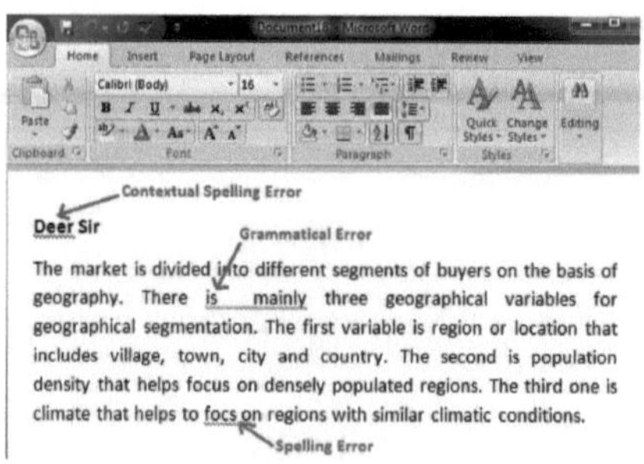


### Steps to correct errors:

- Place the cursor over the text that you want to correct
- Right click the mouse
- A list of suggestions appears
- Choose the correct word with a left click

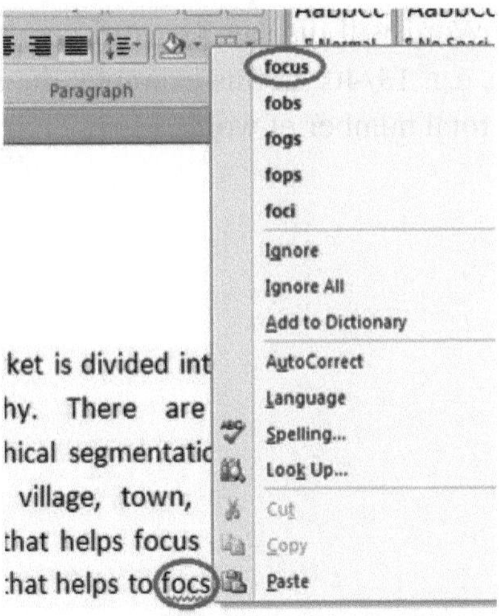


**How to Check Word Count in Ms Word**

When you start typing, the Word automatically counts the number of words and number of pages and displays the information on the status bar. If the word count is not available on the status bar, you can right click the status bar and select the Word Count option from the menu. Basic steps to check the word count are listed below;

- Open the document
- Look at left bottom corner of the document
- You will see the total world count and the number of pages

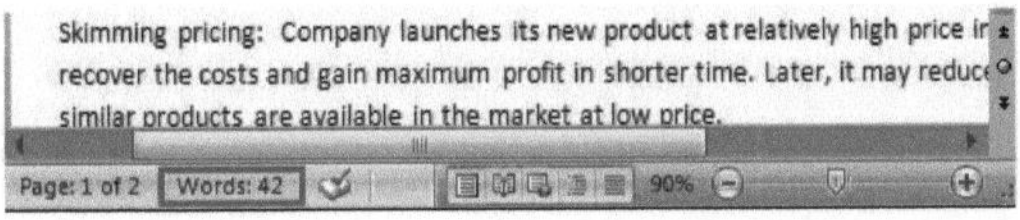

To know the word count of a specific line or paragraph you have to select it then Word will display its word count along with the total word count, e.g. 15/40. In this example, the selection has 15 words out of the total number of words (40).

CHAPTER IV

# Formatting Text

## How to Change Font Size in MS Word

You can easily change the font size of your text in the document. The basic steps to change the Font size are listed below;

- Select the text that you want to modify
- In Home tab locate the Font group
- In Font group click the drop-down arrow next to font size box
- Font size menu appears
- Select the desired font size with a left click
- Select the text and click the increase or decrease font size buttons

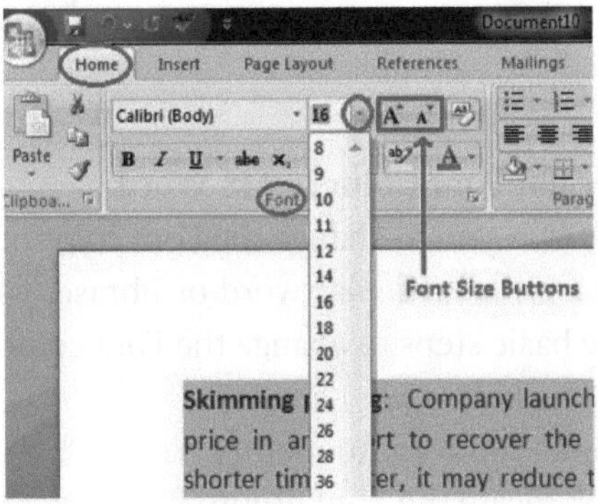


## How to Change Font Style in MS Word

- The basic steps to change the font of a text in a document are given below;
- Select the text you want to modify

- Select the Home tab and locate the Font group
- Click the drop-down arrow next to font style box
- Font style menu appears
- With a left click select the desired font style
- If you want to change the font to bold or italic, click the 'B' or 'I' icons on the format bar.

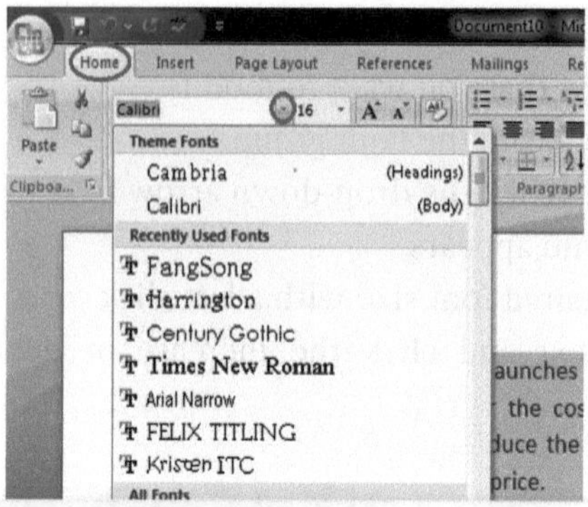


**How to Format Font Color in MS Word**

MS Word allows you to change the Font color of your text. If you want to emphasize a particular word or phrase, you can change its font color. The basic steps to change the Font color are given below;

- Select the text you want to modify
- In Home tab locate the Font group
- Click the drop-down arrow next to Font color button
- Font color menu appears
- Select the desired font color with a left click
- Word will change the Font color of the selected text.

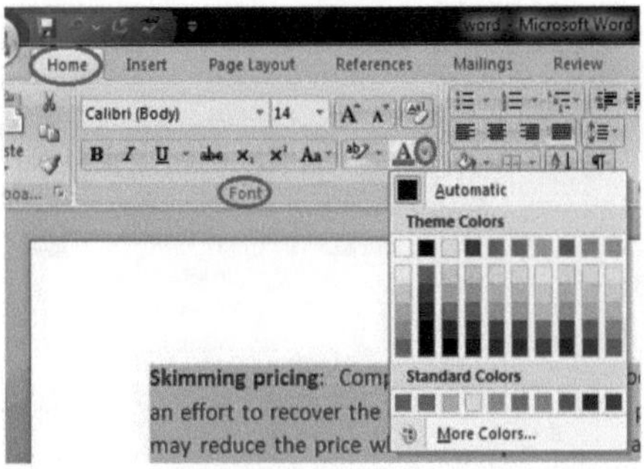


**How to Change Text Case in MS Word**

You can easily change the text case in your document by following the steps given below;

- Select the text you want to change
- In Home tab locate the Font group
- Click the drop-down arrow in 'Change Case' button
- It displays text case menu
- Select the desired case with a left click

The case menu offers four options;

1. Sentence case: It capitalizes the first letter of each sentence.
2. Lowercase: It changes the text from uppercase to lowercase.
3. Uppercase: It capitalizes all the all letters of your text.
4. Capitalize Each Word: It capitalizes the first letter of each word.

Toggle Case: It allows you to shift between two case views, e.g. to shift between Capitalize Each Word and cAPITALIZE eACH wORD

.

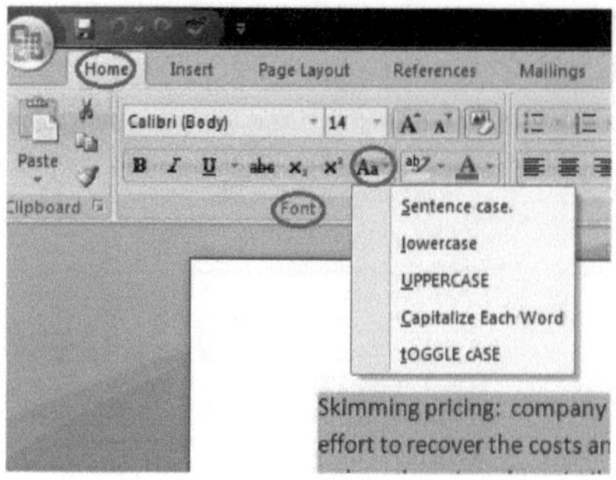


**How to Change Text Alignment in MS Word**

You can change the text alignment in your document to make it more presentable and readable. The basic steps to change the text alignment are given below;

- Select the content you want to modify
- In Home tab locate the Paragraph group
- It has four alignment options ;

1. Align Text Left: Aligns the text towards left margin
2. Center: Brings the text at centre
3. Align Text Right: Aligns the text towards right margin
4. Justify: Aligns the text to both left and right margins

- Select the desired alignment option with a left click

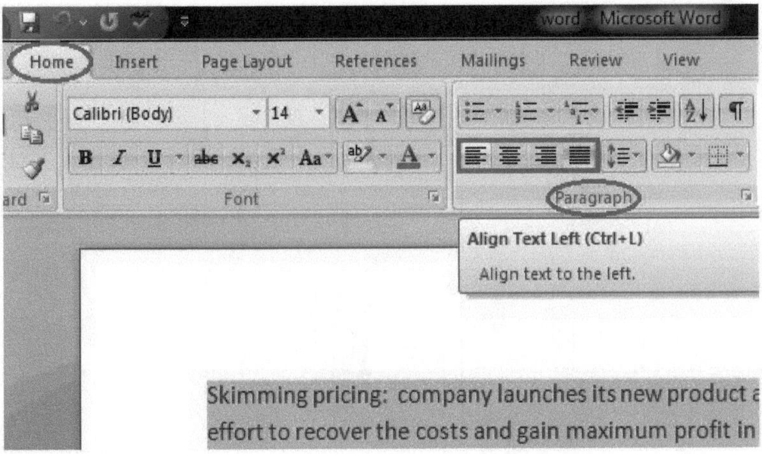


**How to Insert a Text Box in MS Word**

Text box allows you to control the position of a block of text in your document. You can also format them with borders and shading. The two commonly used methods to insert Text Boxes are given below:

Method 1:

- Select the Insert tab
- Locate the Text group
- Click the Text Box button
- It displays Built-In text box menu and an option to draw table
- With a left click select the desired text box format from the menu

Method 2:

- Select 'Draw Text Box' option
- A cross shaped cursor appears
- Left click the mouse and holding it down drag it to draw the box of desired dimensions

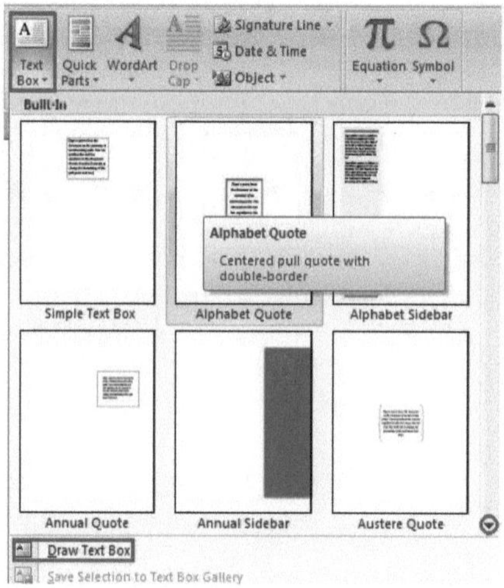


Bold, Italic and Underline Commands in MS Word

These commands are given in the Font group in the Home tab. Their functions are given below;

- Bold: It allows you to Bold the text of your document
- Italic: It allows you to Italicize the text of your document
- Underline: It allows you to underline the text of your document

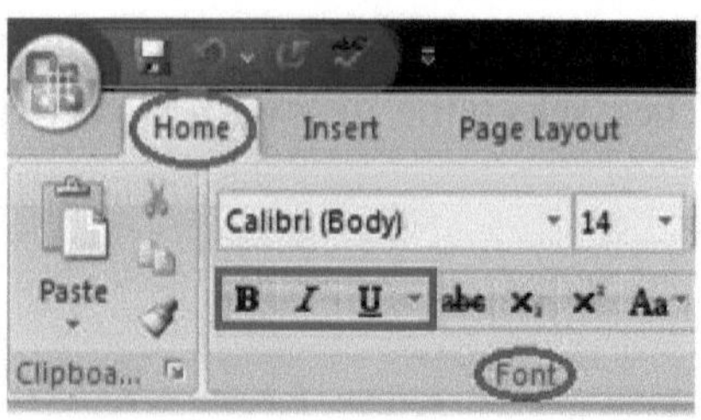

CHAPTER V

# Formatting Paragraph

**How to Create First Line Indent in MS Word**

You can create indent within your paragraph by following these steps;

- Select the paragraph or place the cursor anywhere within the paragraph
- Select the Home tab
- Locate the Paragraph group and click the arrow at right bottom corner
- 'Paragraph' dialog box appears
- In 'Indents and Spacing' section click the drop down arrow in 'Special' field
- Select the 'First Line' option
- Enter desired indent in 'By' field and click Ok

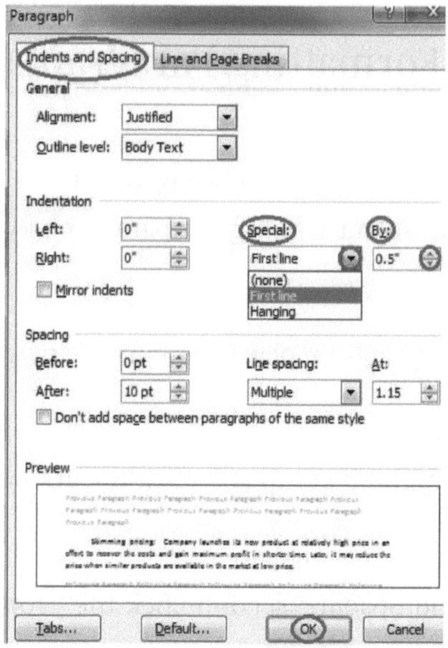


**How to Apply Style in MS Word**

You can create professional and presentable documents in MS Word by applying different styles. The basic steps to apply a style in a document are listed below;

- Select the text to which you want to apply the style
- Select the Home tab
- In Styles group you will see different styles;

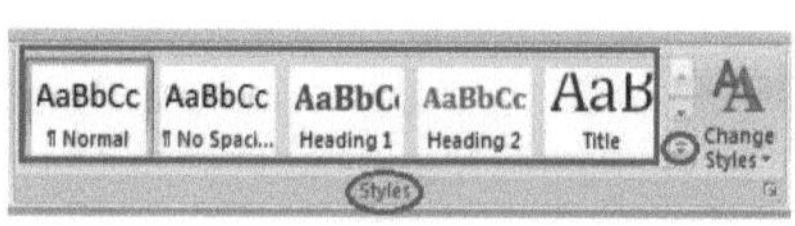

- styles click the drop-down arrow
- It displays style menu
- Select the desired style with a lef

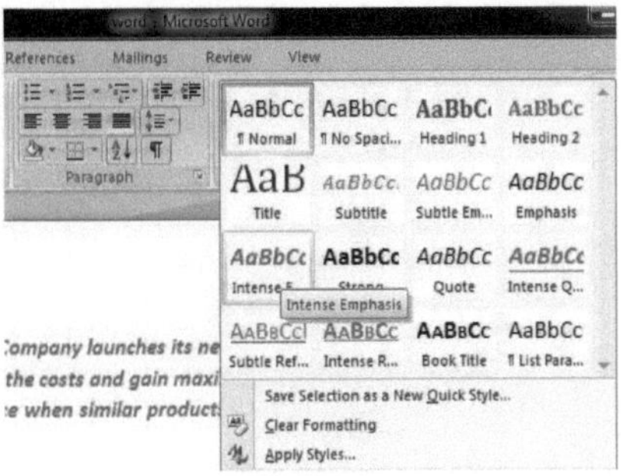


**How to Customize Style in MS Word**

If you are looking for formatting options that are not given in the built-in styles, you can modify or customize an existing style to fulfill your needs. The steps to customize a style are as follows;

- Select the style that you want to modify
- Right click the mouse
- It displays a list of different commands
- Select the 'Modify' option;

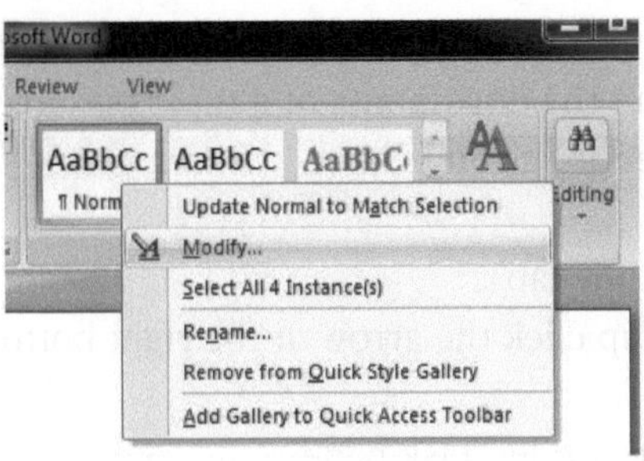

- 'Modify Style' dialogue box appears

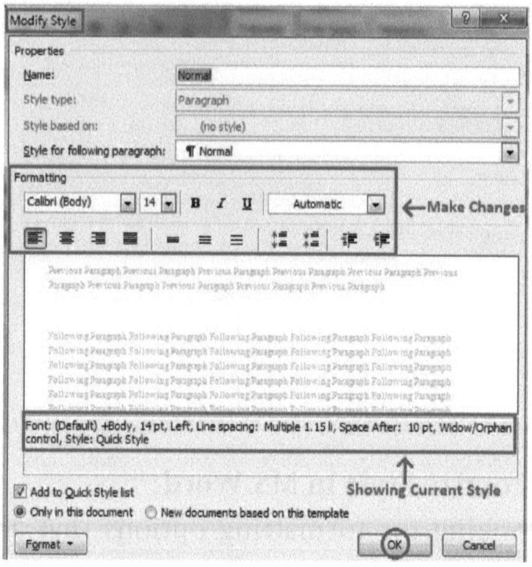


- Make the desired changes to formatting
- Click OK to apply the changes to style

**How to Create New Style in MS Word**

You can add new styles to your list of styles, i.e. Word allows you to set the styles for font, figure, paragraph, etc. It helps you to keep consistency in all the documents of a topic or subject. The steps to create new styles are given below;

- Select the Home tab
- In Styles group click the arrow at the right bottom corner of the group
- It displays the 'Styles' task pane;

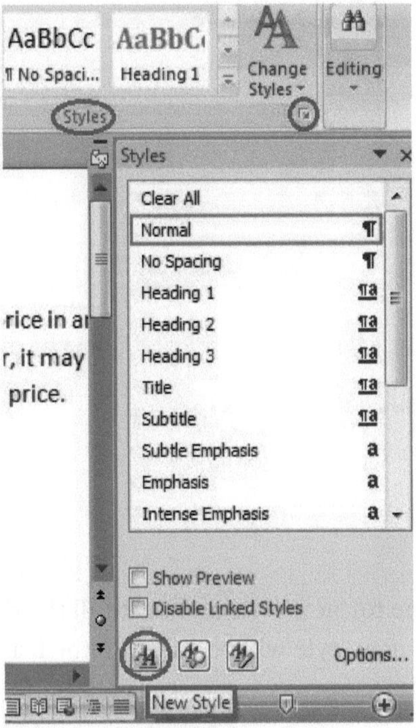


- In 'Styles' task pane click the 'New Style' button
- It displays 'Create New Style from Formatting' dialogue box;

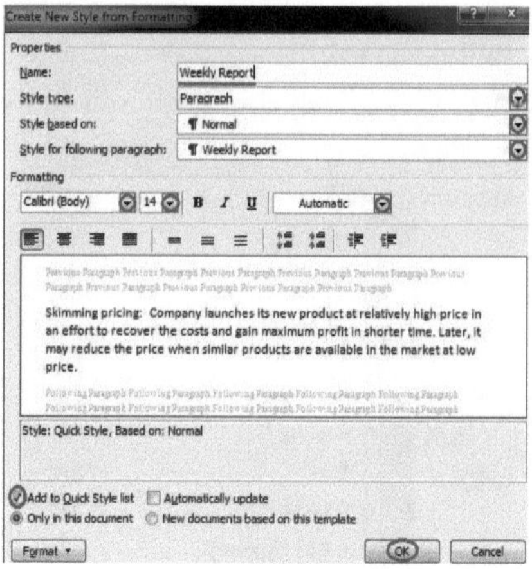


- Enter the name for new style and make all the desired changes
- Click OK, the new style will be added to the list of styles

CHAPTER VI

# Modify Page Layout

**How to Change Page Orientation in MS Word**

Page Orientation refers to the direction in which a document is displayed. It is of two types; portrait (vertical) and landscape (horizontal). The default orientation is portrait; it can be changed to landscape by following these steps;

- Select the Page Layout tab
- Locate the Page Setup group
- In Page Setup group click the Orientation command
- It displays two options, Portrait and Landscape
- Select the desired page orientation

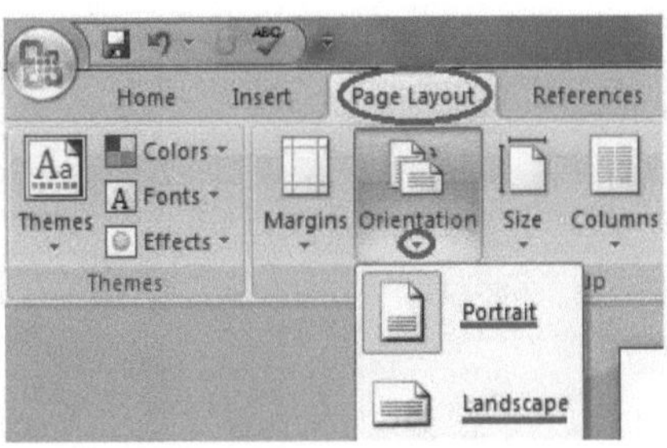


**How to Change Page Size in MS Word**

The default paper size in Word is 8.5 x 11 inches which easily fits in printers. This size is not fixed; you can change it if you want a document with different paper size. The steps to change the paper size are given below;

- Click the Page Layout tab

- In Page Setup group click the Size command
- Paper size menu will appear
- With a left click select the desired paper size
- To customize page size click the 'More Paper Sizes' option

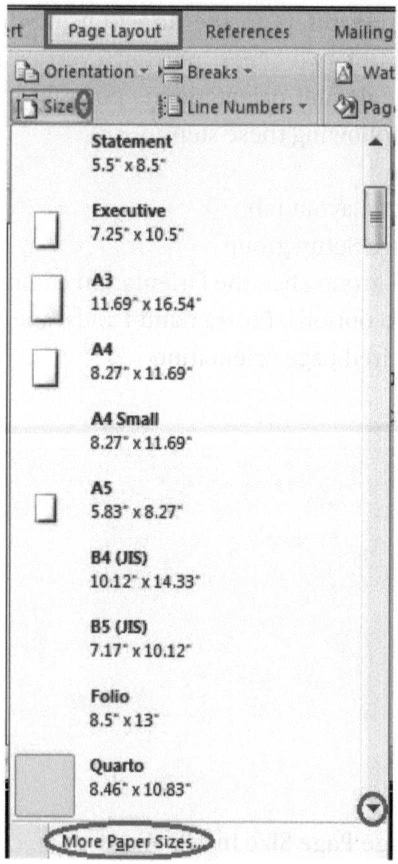


**How to Change Page Margins in MS Word**

The margin is the space between the text and border of a document. By default, it is a one-inch space. Depending on your needs, it can be changed by following the below-listed steps;

- Select the Page Layout tab
- In Page Setup group click the Margins command
- A list of Margins appears
- Select the desired Margin with a left click

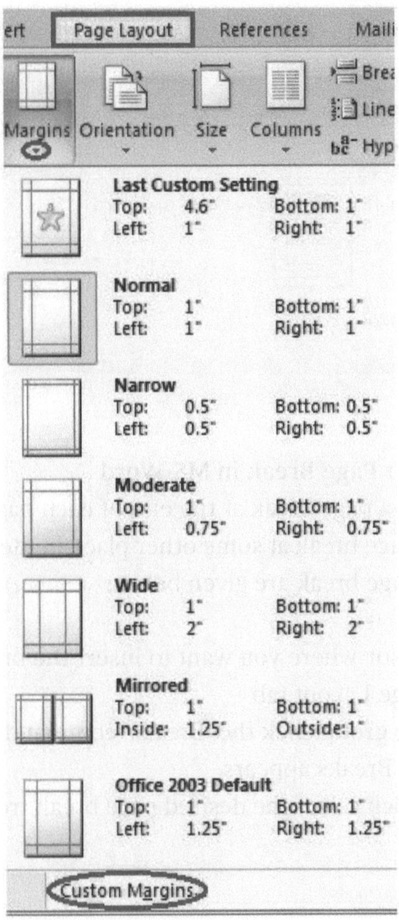


To customize Margins select 'Custom Margins'. It displays a 'Page Setup' dialog box. Enter the desired margin size and click Ok.

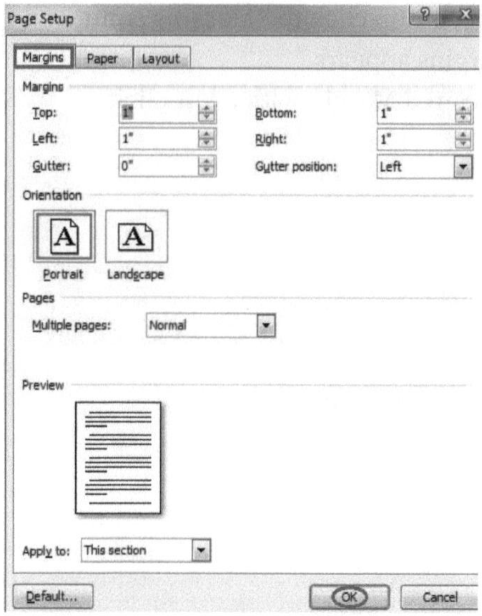


**How to Insert Page Break in MS Word**

Word inserts a page break at the end of each page. It also allows you to insert a page break at some other place in the document. The steps to insert page break are given below;

- Place the cursor where you want to insert the break
- Select the Page Layout tab
- In Page Setup group click the 'Breaks' command
- A list of Page Breaks appears
- With a left click select the desired page break from the list

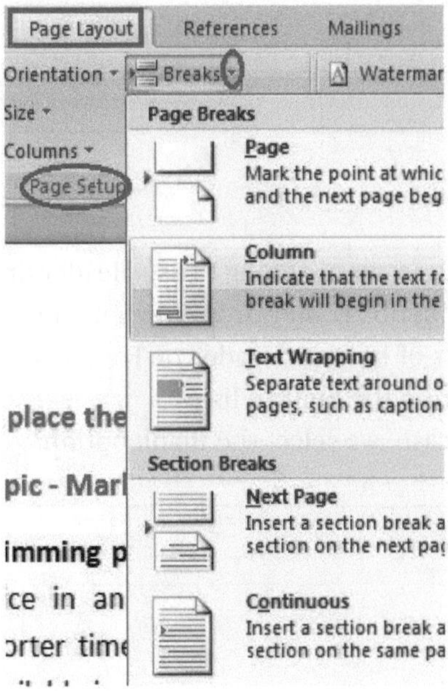


**How to insert a header and footer in Microsoft Word document**

In Microsoft Word, Headers and Footers are used to insert additional information such as title, file name, date, page numbers, etc. The presence of both header and footer in the Word document makes your document more professional and easier to read as well as understand.

Headers appear at the top margin of the Word document, while Footers appear at the bottom margin of the Word document.

To insert a header and footer in Microsoft Word

, follow the below given basic steps -

Step 1: Open the new or an existing Word document in which you want to insert header and footer.

Step 2: Go to the Insert tab at the top of the Ribbon.

Step 3: Click on either header or footer drop-down menu in the Header & Footer section.

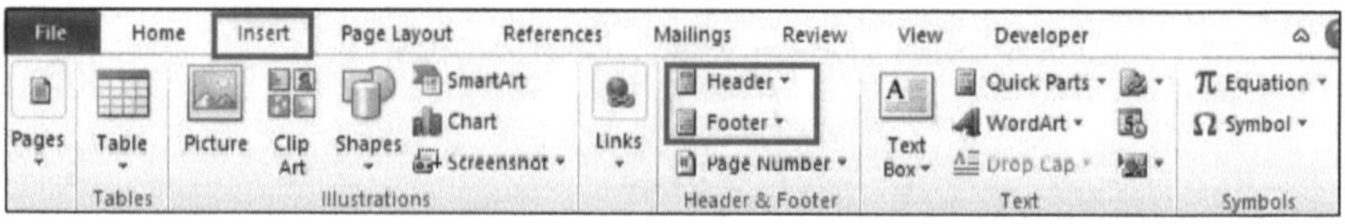


Note: In our case, we are going to use Header drop-down option.

Step 4: A Header or Footer drop-down menu will display on the screen with a list of built-in Header or Footer options. Select your desired option from the Built-in list.

Note: In our case, we select the Blank option.

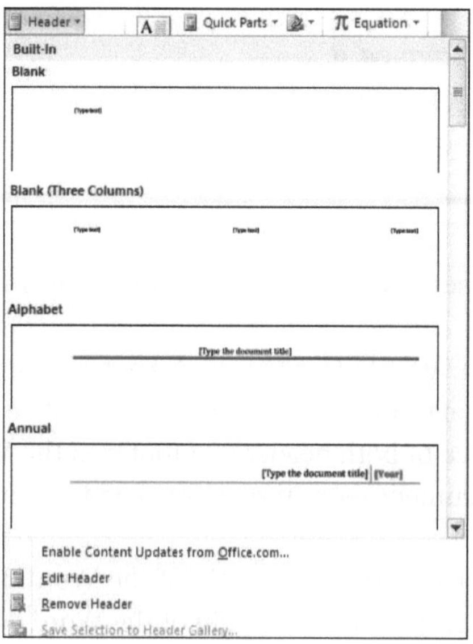


Step 5: A Design tab with Header & Footer option will appear at the top of the document (on the Ribbon), as shown in the below screenshot.

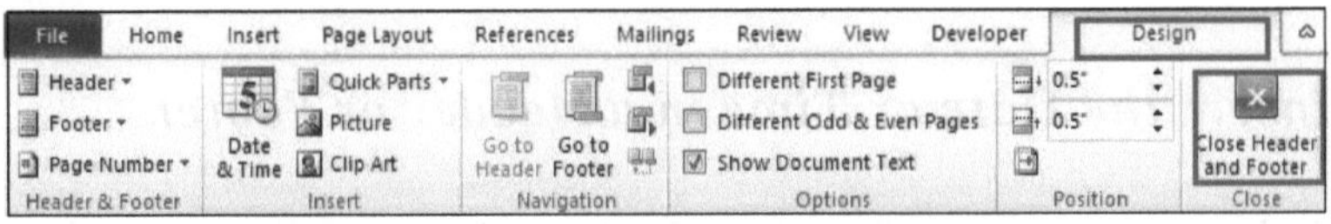


Step 6: Type your desired information into the header or footer section.

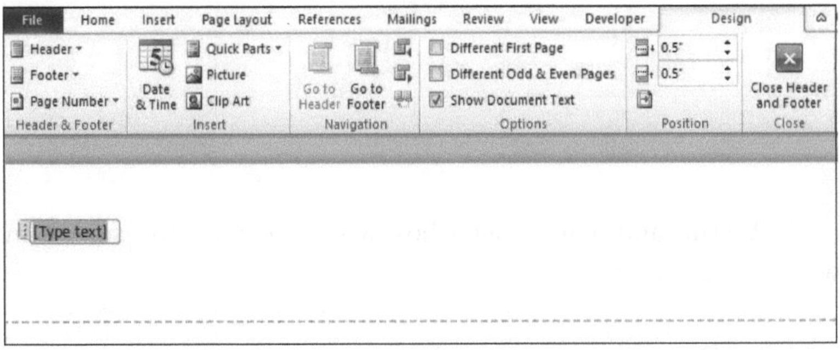


Step 7: Once you type your desired text in the Header section, click on Close Header and Footer under the Design section on the Ribbon or press the Esc key from the keyboard to remove the dotted underline. Now, you can see that the Header is inserted to the Word document.

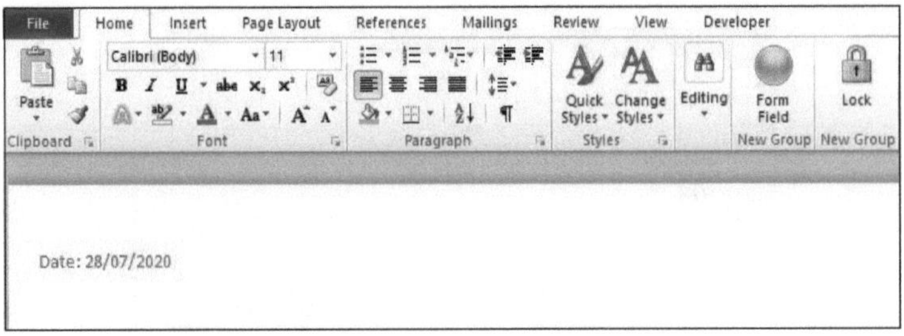

## *Insert the Date or Time in a Header or Footer*

To insert the Date or Time in a Header or Footer, follow the below instructions -

1. Go to the Insert tab on the Ribbon and click on the Date & Time option in the Text section.

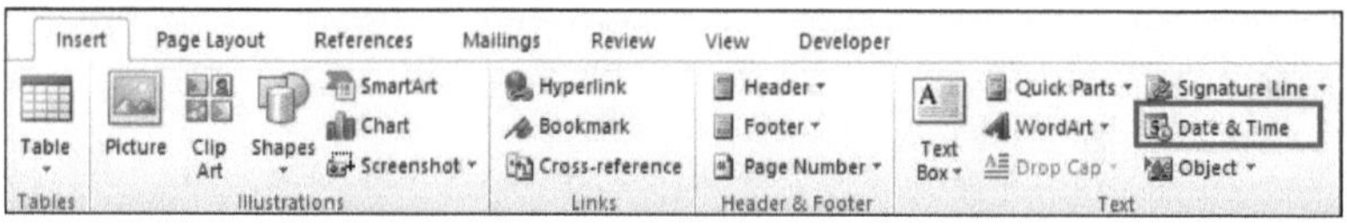


2. A Date and Time dialog box will appear on the screen in which do the following -

- Select Date format from the Available format.
- Select your desired language.
- Tick on the Update automatically checkbox.
- Click on the OK button at the bottom of the dialog box.

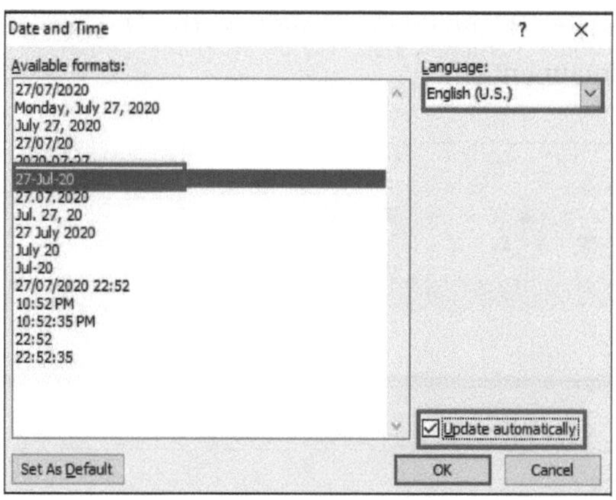

Now, you can see that your selected format will appear on the Word document.

## *Edit Header and Footer in Word document*

Once you create Header and Footer in Word document, you can also edit it based on your requirement.

There are the following steps to edit Header and Footer in Word document.

Step 1: Go to the Insert tab on the Ribbon and click on either Header or Footer drop-down menu that you want to Edit.

Note: In our case, we are going to edit a Header, so we select Header drop-down option.

Step 2: A Built-In Header option window will appear on the screen. Click on the Edit Header option.

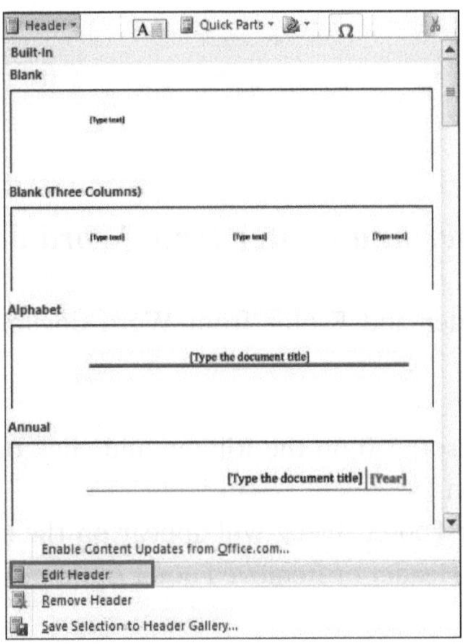

Step 3: Edit Header based on your requirement. Once you edit Header, click on the Close Header and Footer option at the top right corner of the document to disappear the blue dotted lines.

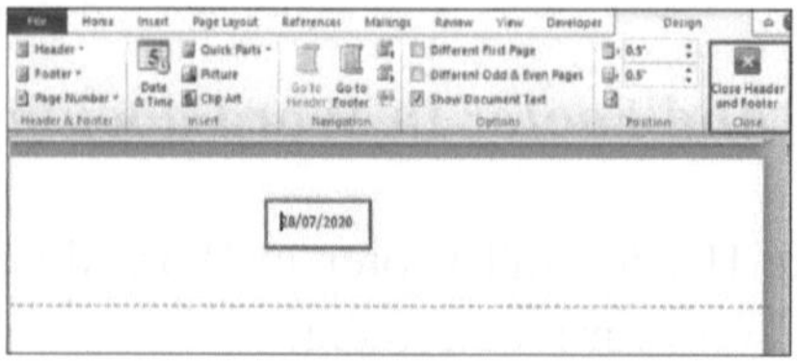

Now, you can see that Header is edit based on your requirement.

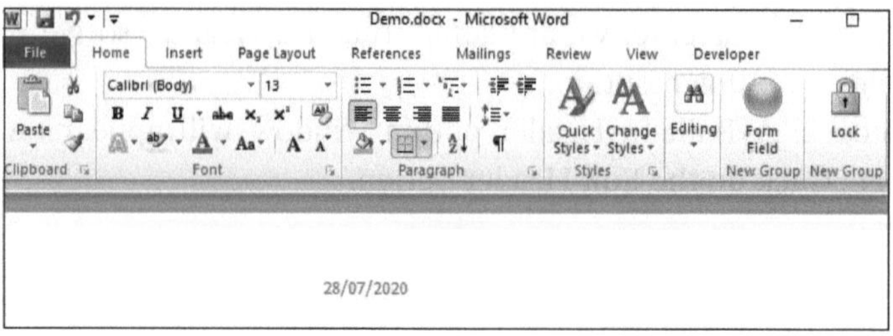


## *Delete Header and Footer from Word document*

To Delete Header and Footer from Word document, follow the below steps -

1. Go to the Insert tab on the Ribbon and click on the Header & Footer option.
2. A Header or Footer dialog will appear on the screen. Click on the Remove Header or Remove Footer option.

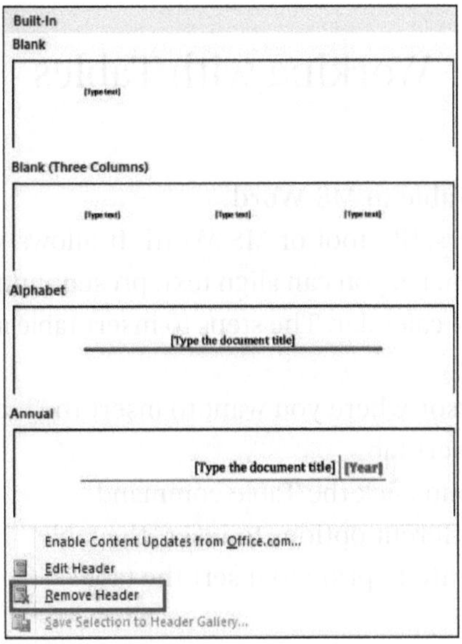
Built-In
Blank
[Type text]
Blank (Three Columns)
[Type text]
[Type text]
[Type text]
Alphabet
[Type the document title]
Annual
[Type the document title]
[Year]
Enable Content Updates from Office.com...
Edit Header
Remove Header
Save Selection to Header Gallery...

CHAPTER VII

# Working with Tables

### How to Insert Table in MS Word

Table is a versatile tool of MS Word. It allows you to organize your information, i.e. you can align text, present numerical data and create forms and calendar. The steps to insert table are given below;

- Place the cursor where you want to insert the table
- Select the Insert tab
- In Tables group click the Table command
- It displays different options to insert the table
- Select the desired option to insert the table

**To Convert Text to Table**

- Select the text
- Select the Insert tab
- In Tables group click the Table command
- Select the 'Convert Text to Table' option;

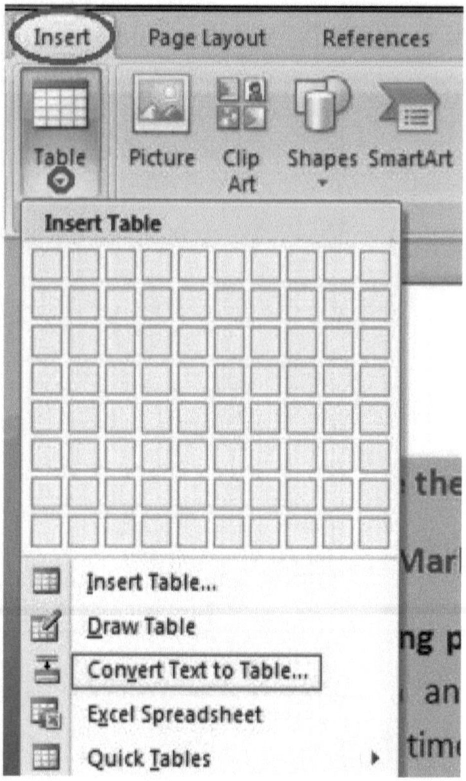


- It displays a dialog box
- In 'Separate text at' section select the desired option
- Click OK, the text will convert to a table

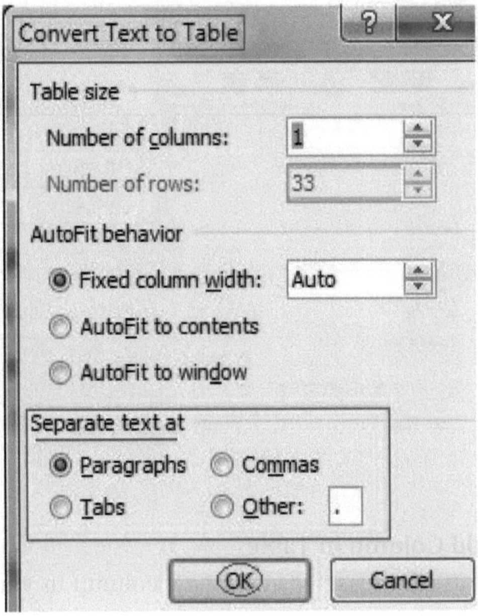


**How to Add Row in Table**

If you want to increase or add a new row in your table, you can follow the steps given below;

- Place the cursor in a row above or below which you want to add row
- Right click the mouse
- A menu appears
- Place the arrow over Insert option
- It will display a menu
- As required select 'Insert Rows Above' or 'Insert Rows Below'

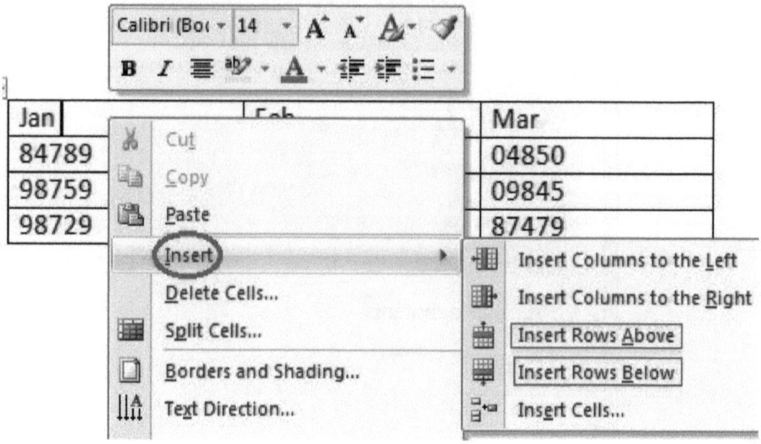


**How to Add Column in Table**

If you want to increase or add a new column in your table, you can follow these steps;

- Place the cursor in the column adjacent to which you want to add the column
- Right click the mouse
- It displays a menu
- Place the arrow over Insert option
- It shows a list of commands
- As required select 'Insert Columns to the Right' or 'Insert Columns to the Left'

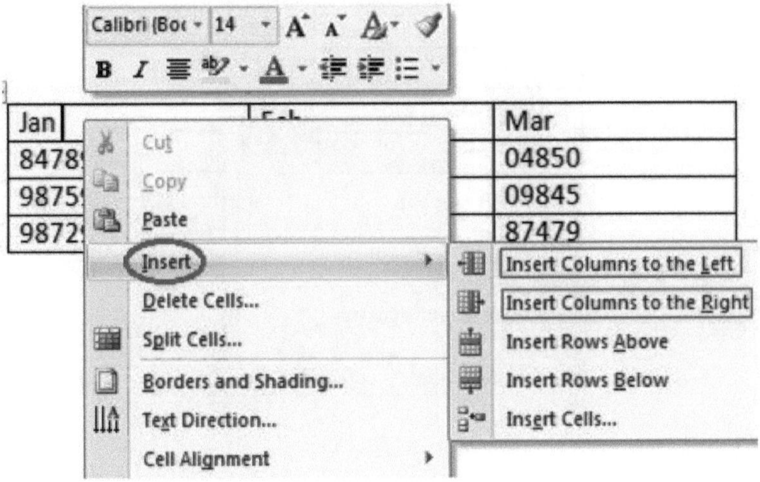


**How to Delete Column or Row in Table**

The table command also allows you to delete a column or row in your table. You can delete the unwanted columns or rows by following these steps;

- Select the column or row of the table
- Right click the mouse
- A menu appears
- As required select 'Delete Columns' or 'Delete Rows'

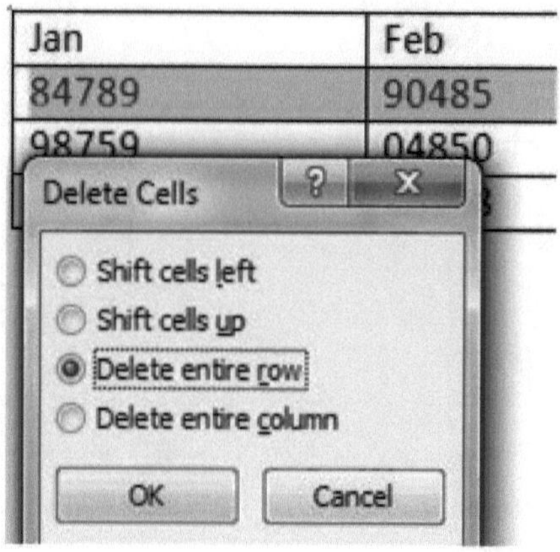


**How to Modify Table**

Word allows you to customize tables as per your requirement. You can modify your table in different ways, i.e. you can choose a table style, table design, draw borders. The steps to modify a table are given below;

- Select the table
- Two new tabs Design and Layout appear on the Ribbon
- On Design tab you will see three groups of commands to modify table; Table Style Options, Table Styles and Draw Borders;

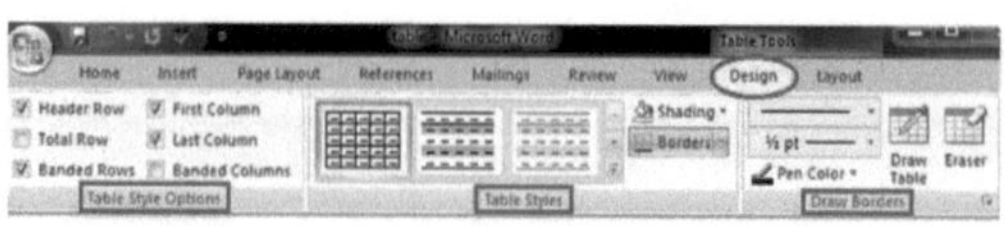

- Layout tab has six groups of commands to format table;

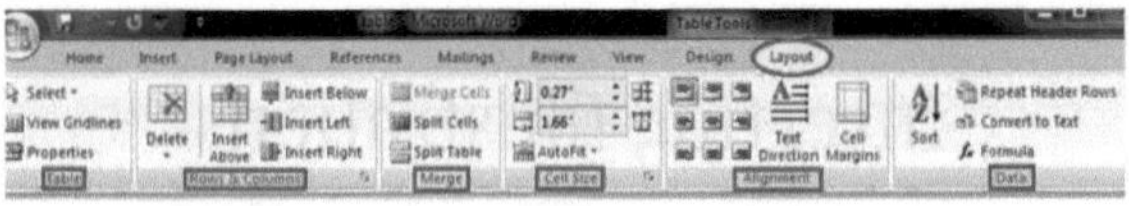

**How to Split Text to Columns**

You can split your text to columns as shown in the image given below. It helps you make your text more readable and presentable. The steps involved in this process are given below;

- Open the document
- Select the Page Layout tab
- In Page Setup group click the Columns command
- It displays a list of options to split text into columns
- Select the desired option

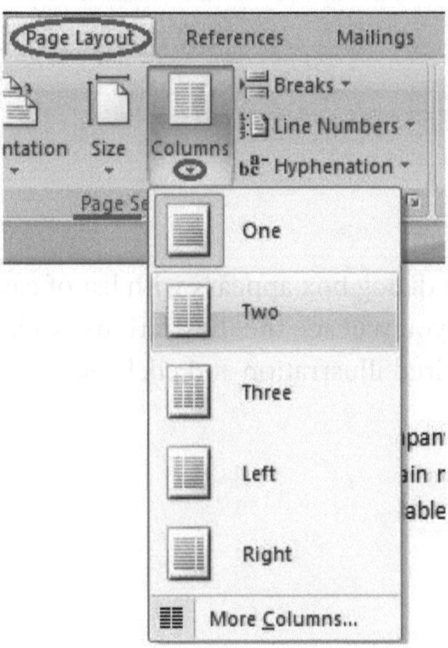

CHAPTER VIII

# Inserting Illustrations

**How to Insert Smart Art Graphics**

You can insert Smart Art Graphics in your document to effectively communicate your message. You can insert a process flow, a relationship or an organization hierarchy. The steps to insert smart art graphics are given below;

- Place the cursor in the document where you want to insert graphics
- Select the Insert tab
- In Illustrations group select the 'Smart Art' command;

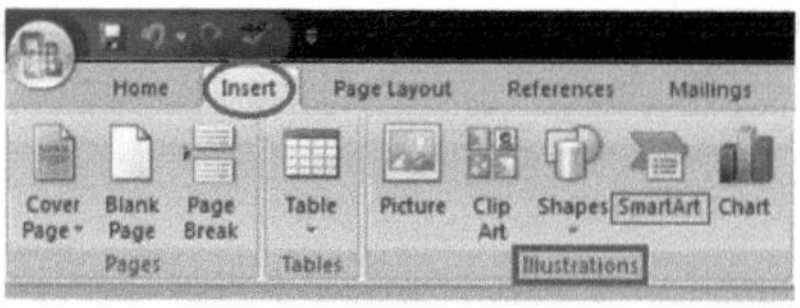


- On left side, a dialog box appears with list of categories
- In the center you will see the illustrations available in a category
- Select the desired illustration and click Ok

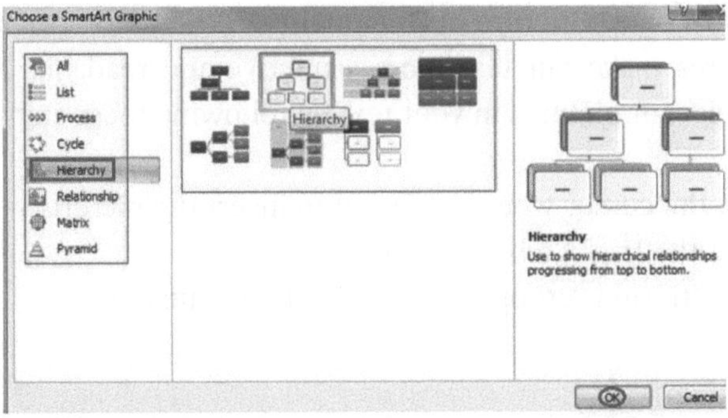


**How to Add Text in Smart Art Graphics**

Word also allows you to add text in Smart Art Graphics; you can add facts, figures and any other information. The steps to add smart art graphics are given below;

- Select the graphic
- Task pane appears on the left side if it is not visible then click the arrow on left side of graphic
- Type the text in task pane fields it will appear in the graphic
- You can also directly type the text in the graphic in text area
- Close the task pane after entering the text and click outside the graphic

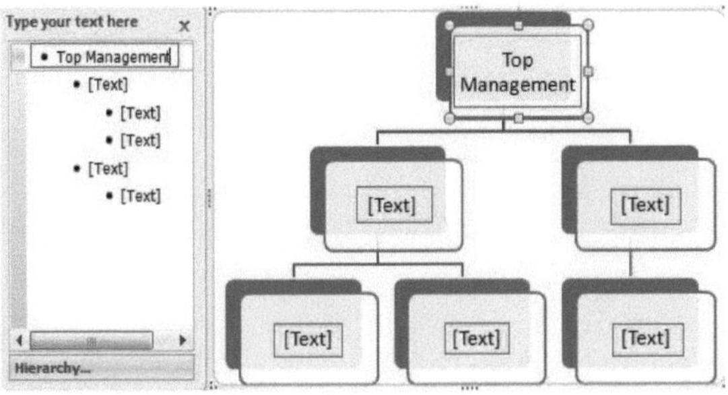

### How to Insert Picture in Document

Pictures make our text more attractive and readable. You can insert relevant pictures in your text by following these steps;

- Place the cursor where you want to insert the picture
- Select the Insert tab on Ribbon
- In Illustrations group click the Picture command;

- It displays 'Insert Picture' dialog box
- Select the desired image
- Click Insert to insert the picture

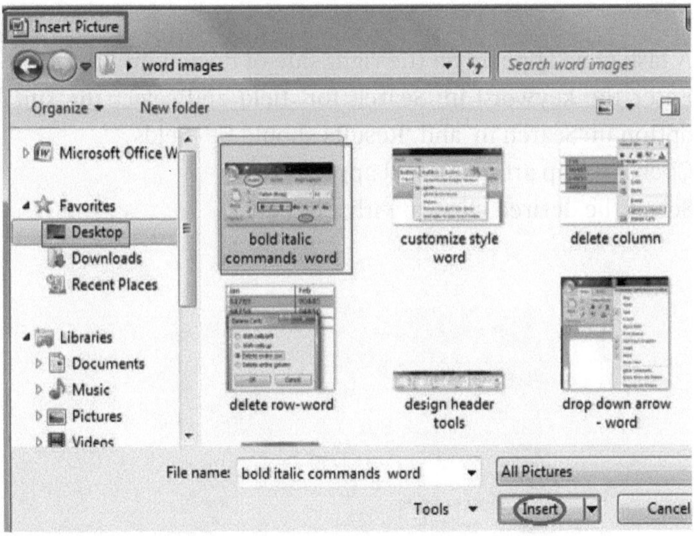


**How to Insert Clip Art**

Clip art refers to a graphic or a picture that you can insert in your document. It comes in different formats and styles. It is used to enhance the appearance of a document. The steps to insert a clip art are given below;

- Place the cursor where you want to insert the clip art
- Select the Insert tab
- In Illustrations group click the Clip Art command;

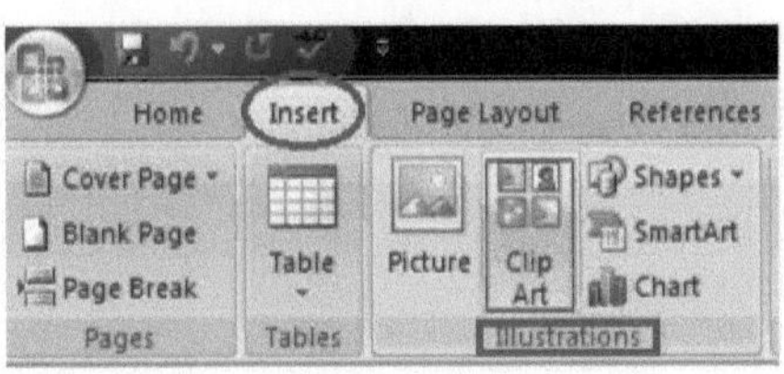

- A task pane appears on the right side of document
- Enter the keyword in 'Search for' field and select the suitable option in 'Search in' and 'Results should be' fields
- Click Go, clip art menu will appear
- Select the desired clip art with a left click

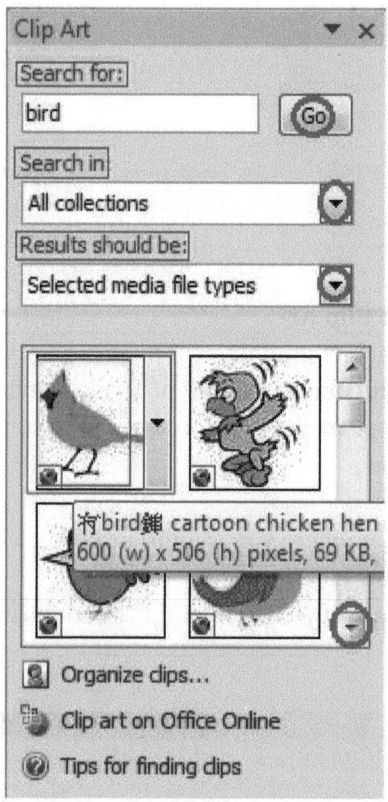


### How to Format Picture or Clip Art

You can change the appearance of your picture or clip art to enhance its visual impact. The format tab offers you various options for formatting pictures like contrast, changing color, line style, cropping, etc. The steps to format picture or clip art are given below;

- Select the picture or clip art that you want to format
- Format tab appears in the Ribbon
- Click the Format tab
- It displays four groups of related commands to modify or format picture or clip art

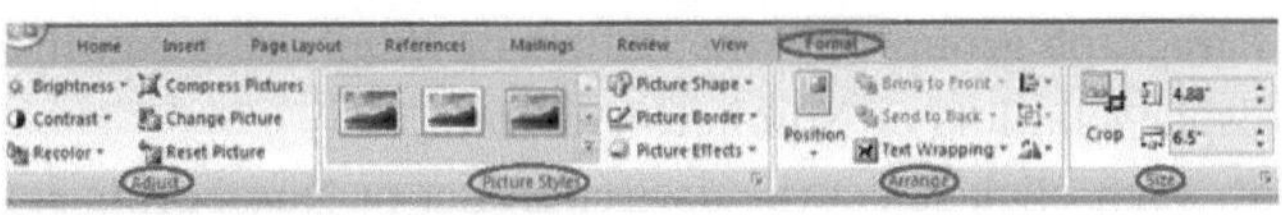

CHAPTER IX

# Working with Lists

## How to Create Bulleted and Numbered Lists

Bullets and numbers are used to make a list more presentable and readable. A bulleted list attracts more than a simple list. Word offers you various styles of bullets and numbers. The steps to create bulleted lists are given below;

- Select the text you want to convert to bulleted or numbered list
- Select the Home tab
- In Paragraph group click the Bullets or Numbering command
- It displays Bullets or Numbering menu
- With a left click select the desired Bullet or Numbering style
- To increase the list place the cursor at the end of list and press Enter key

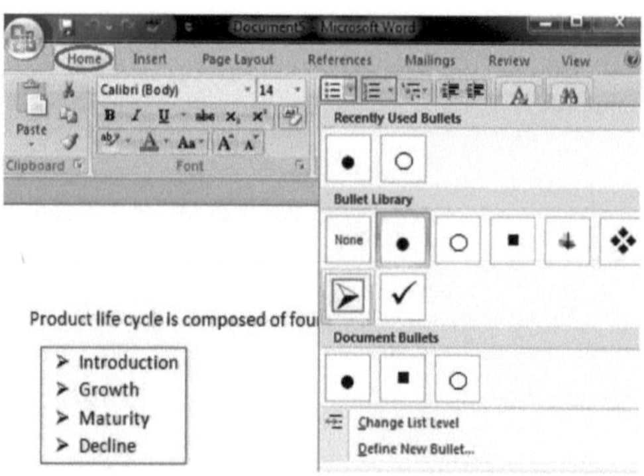


### How to Use Symbols as Bullets

You can replace the bullets with symbols to make your lists more meaningful and attractive. The steps involved in this process are given below;

- Select the text to convert to bulleted list
- Select the Home tab
- In Paragraph group click the Bullets command
- Click 'Define New Bullet' option
- 'Define New Bullet' dialog box appears;

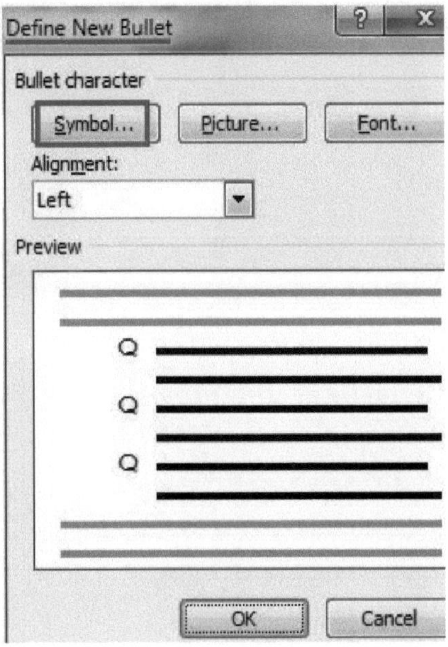


- Click the Symbol command
- It displays 'Symbol' dialog box
- Select the desired symbol
- For more options click the drop down arrow next to Font field

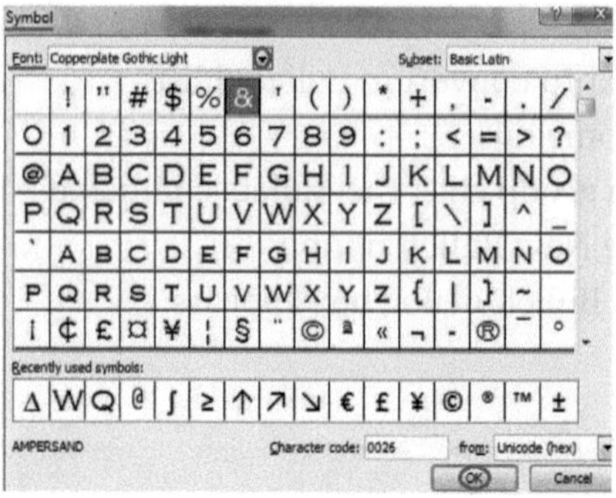
Symbol
Font: Copperplate Gothic Light
Subset: Basic Latin
Recently used symbols:
AMPERSAND
Character code: 0026
from: Unicode (hex)
OK
Cancel

CHAPTER X

# Using WordArt

**How to Insert WordArt**

Word Art is designed to allow you make your text more attractive; you can format your text to make it look like a picture and enhance its appearance in different ways. The steps to insert WordArt are given below;

- Place the cursor where you want to insert WordArt
- Select the Insert tab
- In Text group click the 'WordArt' button
- WordArt menu appears;

- Select the desired WordArt style
- 'Edit WordArt Text' dialog box appears
- Type the text in text area and click OK

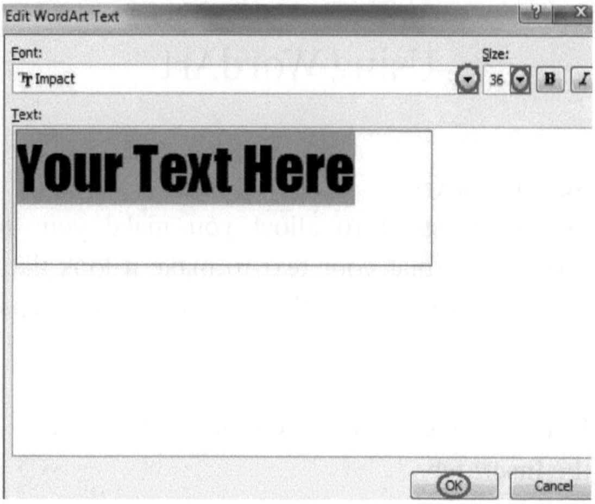


**How to Format WordArt**

Word also allows you to customize WordArt. You can change WordArt shapes, font face and size, and colors as per your requirement. The steps to format WordArt are given below;

- Select the wordart in the document
- Format tab appears in the Ribbon
- It offers five groups of related commands
- Click the suitable command to make desired changes in wordart

9 798887 839097

Printed by Libri Plureos GmbH in Hamburg,
Germany